How to use this book:

We sincerely appreciate your purchase of our meticulously crafted ephemera book. This collection, artfully generated with Ai to serve as a versatile resource for a wide range of creative endeavors, and we'd like to offer some professional and innovative suggestions on how to maximize its potential:

-Papercraft Artistry: Explore the depths of your creativity by using these images to create intricate and captivating papercraft artworks.

-Junk Journaling: For those who love the art of storytelling through visuals, these images are perfect for embellishing your junk journals.

-Scrapbooking Mastery: Elevate your scrapbooking game by incorporating our dark ephemera.

-Decoupage Brilliance: Achieve a seamless blend of vintage and eerie by using these images in your decoupage projects.

-Creative Card Making: Craft unique and memorable cards for any occasion with the help of our dark ephemera.

-Mixed Media Magic: Combine various mediums and techniques to create mixed media artworks that tell hauntingly beautiful stories.

To ensure you make the most of this collection, consider the following tips:

Precise Cutting: When removing images from the book, use sharp, precise cutting tools to maintain the integrity of the designs.

We hope you derive immense joy and satisfaction from working with our dark ephemera. May your creative journey be as enchanting as the images themselves.

Happy crafting!

TEEDRY